All Y...

Psychic Development

Ravindra Kumar, Ph D
(Swami Atmananda)

New Dawn

NEW DAWN
An imprint of Sterling Publishers (P) Ltd.
A-59 Okhla Industrial Area, Phase-II, New Delhi-110020.
Tel: 6912677, 6910050, 6916165, 6916209
Fax: 91-11-6331241 E-mail: ghai@nde.vsnl.net.in
www.sterlingpublishers.com

All You Wanted to Know About - Psychic Development
©2001, Sterling Publishers Private Limited
ISBN 81 207 2367 8

Reprint 2002

Published by Sterling Publishers Pvt. Ltd., New Delhi-110016.
Lasertypeset by Vikas Compographics, New Delhi-110029.
Printed at Shagun Composer New Delhi-110029.

Contents

Preface

Psychic development implies 'evolution' that is accompanied by acquisition of senses and powers beyond the five normal senses of hearing, seeing, smelling, tasting and touching. With the opening of the chakras, the hitherto dormant regions of the brain awaken gradually. With these awakenings, the individual acquires powers such as clairvoyance, clairaudience, telepathy, prophecy, levitation, out-of-body experiences, healing, etc., depending on one's training and interests. People known for their outstanding achievements in any field, have been successful because they were able to develop the psychic potential within them. Any one, ranging from a carpenter to a social reformer, can achieve success by developing the psychic potential, that lies within.

The theory of psychic development is presented in this book. The text is based on personal experiences of people, especially those associated with The Academy of Kundalini Yoga and Quantum

Soul. It is a complete guide for a lay person who wants to learn to harness his or her energies in a really productive way. Thanks are due to William Henry Belk II for discussing various aspects of this book with me and to Jytte Larsen for participating in spiritual discussions, and for providing computing facilities.

Introduction

The psychic phenomenon is related to the spiritual nature, ie., the soul of the human being. This was also the observation of a famous psychic Edgar Cayce, who did thousands of readings on the past lives of humans. In the later years, the psychic ability of Edgar Cayce was so developed that the moment he looked at a person, he would know the circumstances he or she was passing through and what was going to happen in the future.

Sitting in a restaurant he told a waitress he had never seen before, that she should not marry the person she was going around with at that time, otherwise she would repeat the mistake she had already committed with her two former husbands. This ability to see the future is called *psychic hunch*. Saint Ramakrishna could keep track of his disciples psychically while they were travelling. Many dignitaries such as Julius Caesar, Abraham Lincoln, John F. Kennedy, Indira Gandhi, etc., were warned of their approaching assassinations by people who had *psychic premonition*. Emanuel Swedenborg saw his neighbour's house on fire psychically, while he was sitting some four hundred miles away. Many people described the exact scene of the Titanic disaster four days before it happened. Just when the invincible ship 'Titanic' was leaving the Southampton docks in England, some people psychically saw the Titanic disaster in advance. St. Paul was forewarned of being arrested on entering Jerusalem by his friends, who foresaw it happening psychically. For more details one can refer to my book *Destiny, Science and Spiritual Awakening* (1997).

Other vital examples of psychic development include *psychic surgery* and *distance healing*. Healers from the Philippines and Brazil have been quite well-known. Tony Agpaoa of the Philippines was known to treat nearly 300 patients in a day. In psychic surgery, you do not use any anaesthesia to remove a defective part of the body such as a kidney, or an unwanted cancerous growth. Instead, you remove the defective part simply by inserting your hand inside the body of the patient. In about a minute or two the operation is over, there is no sign of any wound and you can just wipe the blood stains with a piece of cloth. I met two individuals in North Carolina who had undergone this kind of operation successfully.

These phenomena do not have a scientific explanation. On other levels you have 'near death' and 'out-of-body' experiences, in which the soul comes out of the body and watches everything from outside. A woman parachutist could not open her parachute and was panicky on seeing her imminent death. Her soul came out of her body, realised the mistake (that she had not pressed a particular button), returned to the body to press that button, and she finally landed safely on the ground as the parachute opened up. But now, she was not the same person; she had seen the ultimate reality and so she took to serious meditation to achieve that state permanently.

On a higher level, yogis have been experiencing these phenomena, which have always defied science for thousands of years. Even science might reach that level one day, but it will take a long time. Yogis die while living in their states of meditation, and report of phenomena that are *psychic* in nature. In China, some people were known to have read books through their fingers. These happenings are beyond the five normal senses of perception.

Duke University in USA has a department of parapsychology, established by Professor J.B.Rhine in 1920, where regular experiments are conducted on such phenomena. You can watch the feats of telekinesis in which a person can move objects or twist things without the use of any visible force. You can also see experiments on levitation, telepathy, precognition, etc., for which researchers have not been able to find a scientific explanation. Various examples of 'psychic phenomena' are studied in a systematic way in this book.

Defining
Psychic Phenomena

The phenomena related to the five physical senses — of hearing, seeing, smelling, tasting and touching belong to the conscious world; these are called 'physical phenomena'. There are other phenomena which are found to be beyond these five senses, that is, they are not perceived through these five senses; these are called 'psychic phenomena'. Every human being lives in two kinds of realities:

conscious and subconscious. Physical phenomena belong to conscious reality, and include activities such as walking, eating, speaking, hearing, mating, etc. Psychic phenomena belong to the field of subconscious reality, comprising experiences such as dreams, visions, hunches, precognition, telepathy, clairvoyance, clairaudience, etc. There are other states of being, such as being under the influence of drugs or medicines, having a fever, etc., in which human beings become connected with the subconscious reality. This is evident from the fact that people report seeing and feeling things in delirium, which are impossible in conscious reality. Such happenings also come under the category of psychic phenomena.

Data collected from the Egyptian Book of the Dead, the Tibetan Book of the Dead, Theosophical Society, experiments of Dr Ian Stevenson, past life readings of Edgar Cayce, experiences of saints and yogis all over the world, etc., suggest that there is a psychic world beyond the physical world, where psychic phenomena are common. Under certain conditions, people are seen to exhibit psychic experiences in the physical realms, which shows that somehow their self has been connected to the subconscious or psychic reality, temporarily. The moment that connection is severed, they behave as normal human beings. There exists, therefore, some switching system which connects the self to the subconscious or psychic reality for some time. Certain yogis who are adepts in these psychic phenomena, such as the present-day Sai Baba, have the knowledge of this 'switching system²; and they can put this switch on whenever they like, or perhaps, they have this switch on permanently.

We have an excellent example of an individual called Peter Hurcos, sponsored by William Henry Belk II of North Carolina, who had also sponsored me. Once Peter fell down from a staircase and his head hit the ground. He was unconscious for some time and when he regained consciousness, he found that he had developed the psychic power of clairvoyance, that is, he could see things happening in any part of the world by simply closing his eyes and concentrating. When the US government came to know of his power, the US police department requested his help to locate criminals through his clairvoyant power. For several years he helped the police in arresting many hardened criminals. He would concentrate and see the person concerned in his mind, and would give the address to the police. In whatever part of the country the criminal was, the local police managed to arrest him in no time.

Today there are a large number of people who advertise as clairvoyants and charge money for their services. This illustrates the use of psychic powers for material gains. There are others who can see your aura and tell about your physical, mental, emotional and spiritual well-being. One can see an aura only after developing the requisite psychic power. People can also tell you to what extent your particular chakras are open by hanging a pendulum on your body and observing its rotations. If the chakra is wide open, the pendulum will move at great speed in a circular motion, making large circles. If the chakra is closed, the pendulum will remain still.

There are a large number of mediums these days who possess psychic powers. Only about two decades ago there was a man by the name of Daniel Dunglas Home in Scotland who could stretch or contract his body up to 11 inches. Stretching or contracting the body is another example of psychic ability. Then there have been many cases in which people could attain weightlessness and could fly in the air for some time, for example, St Teresa of Avila. This, too, is a psychic phenomenon.

I believe the readers have now clearly understood what a psychic phenomenon is. We will now define some of the well-known psychic or paranormal powers in the following chapters.

Defining Psychic Powers

There are a large number of phenomena which can be categorised as psychic. However, we are going to explain and define some of them, which are common.

Extrasensory Perception (ESP)
It could very well be thought of as synonymous with psychic phenomenon or sixth sense, since the information is perceived without the use of the five senses of hearing, seeing, smelling, tasting and touching. ESP is a term coined by

parapsychologists for the purpose of research. In 1920, Dr J.B.Rhine established a department to research on the phenomenon of ESP, at the Duke University in North Carolina and hence, now we have enough evidence of its existence. Clairvoyance and telepathy are the two main divisions, both of which take us towards precognition and retrocognition. Science has no formulae to explain these phenomena. To me it is like measuring the infinite with a finite yardstick. Brain (physical) and mind (consciousness) are two different things. Quantum physics has admitted the existence of another reality, which can be called the 'non-material universe'. The West is slowly accepting this Eastern concept, that the phenomenon of ESP belongs to another reality.

Dr Carl Jung said that the conscious mind could psychically contact the 'collective sub-conscious', which is the universal storehouse of the past, present and future. However, until the information filters in from the subconscious to the conscious, the individual is not aware of it.

Sometimes it gets mixed with the blockages and distortions of the conscious mind and results in inaccuracies. People who are relaxed, intuitive and believe in the existence of the other world, get clearer ESPs than the ones who are analytical, skeptical and tensed. The evidence suggests that the gift of ESP is inherited rather than acquired, as we have seen in numerous cases of saints and prophets. Yet, others believe that almost everyone has it to some extent and it is more prominent in childhood; it slowly fades away

Prayer of Renunciation of Satan

In the name of the Lord Jesus Christ I renounce all the workings of Satan in my life in all its forms, whether brought into my life by my actions or by others.

I break all attachments, ground, curses, spells, malefice, evil eye, and rights Satan may have in my life whether such ground was gained through my actions or through others.

Strengthened by the intercession of the Immaculate Virgin Mary, Mother of God, Blessed Michael the Archangel, the Blessed Apostles Peter and Paul, and all the Saints and Angels of Heaven, and powerful in the holy authority of the name of the Lord Jesus Christ, I ask you Lord to command Satan and all his minions, whomever they may be, to get out of my life and stay out.

With that authority I now take back the ground in my life gained by Satan through my sins. I reclaim this ground and my life for Christ. I now dedicate myself to the Lord Jesus Christ; I belong to Him alone. Amen.

with the acquirement of worldly knowledge. This view is supported by the fact that the cases of 'past life memories' are generally seen in early childhood, and are forgotten by the time the child reaches adolescence. According to a survey, most people have at least one ESP experience in their lifetime.

Louisa E. Rhine researched 10,000 cases and concluded that ESP occurs in four ways: realistic dreams, intuition, unrealistic dreams and hallucinations. Realistic dreams are the best and most common means, as they contain maximum details. This is so because the barriers and blockages of the conscious mind are not present in the dream. Cases of negative information such as accidents, deaths and disasters are larger than those of positive and happy information. Perhaps the subliminal barriers are easily broken in cases of shocks and traumas. Divisions of ESP are now discussed one by one.

Clairvoyance

It is the property of seeing an event taking place far away from the subject, through his or her mind, without the aid of any physical means. Jeanne Dixon, through her precognitive clairvoyance, saw the scenes of assassinations of John F. Kennedy, Robert Kennedy and Martin Luther King, and gave them warnings well in advance, though either none of them believed her or they could not heed these warnings, for one reason or the other. Emanuel Swedenborg saw the raging fire which engulfed the house of his neighbour some 300 miles away, exactly at the time of its happening, as confirmed later by the witnesses. Mrs. Nella Jones saw in advance the scenes of murder committed by the

Yorkshire Ripper, which was responsible for his identification later. I remember having seen the clairvoyant feats of magicians on the streets in India, in which they could tell the correct registration number of an approaching vehicle which was a fair distance away at that time. They could also correctly tell the numbers on the currency notes any one was carrying in his or her pocket. The Titanic disaster was clairvoyantly seen four days before it took place, by a housewife who was watching the launching of the ship from the top of her house in Southampton.

Clairvoyance results from yogic practices when the sixth chakra (between the eyebrows) opens up, and it is called a *siddhi*. The degree of clairvoyance varies from person to person, according to the level of development. At the lowest level, people see images of symbols, which are to be interpreted for their meanings. At the highest level, people see planes of higher realms — astral, mental, causal, etc., and the inhabitants of those realms such as the demons or demi-gods, as the case may be. In mystical states people see angelic beings on higher planes. These are known as spiritual worlds and are seen by yogis on the opening of the third eye. However, the third eye generally opens for a specific period only, and then it closes down. It gives a glimpse of the goal to be achieved. Perhaps the high order yogis have their spiritual eye permanently open. I have described my own experiences of having seen spiritual worlds in my books *Destiny, Science and Spiritual Awakening* (1997) and *Kundalini – An Autobiographical Guide to Self/God Realisation (1999).*

Many mediums such as Edgar Cayce, have been able to read *akashic* records of persons clairvoyantly and advise them accordingly. Those who can see the auras of people also possess the clairvoyant property. In 'dream clairvoyance' people dream of an event, which is either taking place at the same time, or which is scheduled to take place in the near future. Such dreams of future events may either give precognitive warnings of possible mishaps in life, or advance knowledge of the spiritual life one is going to live after death, as the case may be.

Clairaudience

It is the property of hearing voices, music or sounds of different kinds through inner ears, which is not possible normally. It manifests as an inner sound or voice, quite different from one's own inner sound or voice. People may recognise it as the sound of a dead relative or demi-god or their spirit-guide. In higher, developed states, the sound is perceived as external. Highly creative individuals and great persons have always reported hearing clairaudiently.

In yogic practices it is known as a *siddhi* and it manifests when the fifth chakra or throat centre opens up. There are various kinds of sounds that one hears; it could be the roaring of a lion, sound of a water - fall, tinkling of bells, buzzing of bees, a single note of the flute, sound of a thousand violins at a distance, sound of woodwinds, the vibrations of a high tension wire or a cool breeze, etc. Different sounds correspond to different levels of evolutionary perfection. In the highest state one hears the sound of *Om* or *Logos* or the *Word*, which is the creative faculty of God.

It was early morning (around 2 a.m.) on July 1987 in Zimbabwe when I got up and heard a sound hitherto unknown. On making enquiries, I was told that no one else could hear any such sound. Next morning I went to an ENT specialist, who said that there was nothing medically wrong with me. I was a little afraid until about one year later, when I came to know of the reality. Although I have been hearing many other sounds from time to time, the sound I heard in 1987 has permanently been echoing in my inner ears till today. In fact, its note and clarity have increased with time.

Demons, guardian spirits or angels have reportedly spoken to important people at crucial moments. According to the *Bible*, King Solomon heard the voice of the Lord telling him that he was a special and unique person. Joan of Arc distinctly heard the voices of her guiding spirits — Michael, Margaret and Catherine. Socrates used to hear a spirit speaking to him, especially at the time of a crisis. The only exception was when he was sentenced to death, which is why he did not run away. However, not all cases of clairaudience are important. In cases where mediums talk to the dead relatives of the audience, in cases of psychic readings and in the experiences of *shamans*, clairaudient voices are usually heard.

Precognition

It is the foreknowledge of the future, obtained directly without the use of the five physical senses. It is the most common of all ESP experiences, and in most cases it is perceived through dreams. Other means of precognition are day visions, intuitive thoughts, whispering in ears, sixth sense, through mediums, divination and trances.

A study by J.W.Dunne (1927) showed that most people have precognitive dreams but they do not realise it, do not remember the details and cannot interpret the symbols occurring in their dreams. Professor J.B.Rhine, Louisa Rhine and their research team at the Duke University came across the phenomena of precognition and psychokinesis while experimenting with ESP cards for telepathy in the 1920s and 1930s.

As mentioned earlier, the assassinations of many important persons were seen in advance by a large number of people. In some cases the victims themselves had precognitive dreams or hunches about their deaths, for example, Abraham Lincoln and Indira Gandhi both had intuitions about their imminent deaths. Religious scriptures of almost all faiths and traditions are full of precognitive instances, in one form or the other. In present-day life too, instances like the foreseeing of the Titanic disaster suggest that people can see future happenings in advance. In 1898, Morgan Robertson wrote a novel *Futility*, which is about the sinking of a ship. The details of the mishap tally more than 90 per cent with the details of the Titanic disaster, which took place on April 15, 1912. Was it not a case of precognition by Robertson, some 14 years before the occurring of the event?

The question that arises now is about 'free will'; do we have it or not? Greeks and many others around the globe believe that the future is immutable, which means that you have seen the effects even before the causes have come into action. According to quantum physics this is possible. However, research has shown that the 'precognated future' is perhaps the 'strongest possible outcome', based on the present trend of events, if it continues to be so. If by the application of free will or otherwise, the present trend of events can be changed, the real happenings in the future may differ from the predicted future. Nevertheless our habits have become so hardened over the years, that we cannot change our ways of living, even if we try. And that is why we are predictable. Even so, in quantum physics, an electron on being disturbed from its path of rotation has the free will to choose a new path of rotation; but invariably it chooses the same old path because it is familiar and easy. This explains how or why precognition works.

Some four hundred years ago, Nostradamus predicted the wiping out of a major part of the population of the world due to a war in 1999. Most of his predictions made earlier came true, so what about this one? I would say that he was not completely wrong since many a time in 1999, we felt that things would happen anytime as he had predicted. Perhaps peaceful efforts of the United Nations saved the situation by controlling and changing the trend of events. And who knows, if the weapons of mass destruction are under production, the prediction may still come true, with a little difference on the scale of time.

I will conclude this section by saying that precognition is an art or talent, which can be developed by the methods we are going to discuss in the next chapter. I have been getting precognitive dreams all my life, especially at the time of some crisis or some good development. For example, dreaming of receiving fruits or flowers has always brought me an appointment letter or news of getting a job, within a few days of having seen the dream. Seeing a pair of things in a dream has brought a situation of confusion or indecision. Dreaming of dogs chasing me or trying to bite me has often been followed by disputes with relatives regarding property matters. Seeing myself naked in a dream has been an indication of negative or harmful circumstances in official life, resulting in some kind of loss. Lately, dreaming of snakes or lotuses has been a pre-indication of opening of a chakra. With regular practice one can prepare one's own dictionary of dreams, which can prove quite useful. Evidence suggests that a dream normally materialises within 24 to 48 hours. However, dreams may take weeks, months or even years before they materialise.

Telepathy

It is the ability to communicate with another person without the use of the physical senses. Ideas, thoughts, feelings and images get transferred mentally without the use of any physical means. Frederic W. H. Myers of Britain coined the word 'telepathy' in 1882. It has its origin in the Greek language: tele — distant, pathe — occurrence. Sigmund Freud, Carl Jung and William James encountered this phenomenon in one way or the other. The Society for Psychical Research in Britain (1884) and the American Society for Psychical Research in the USA (1885) were specially founded to investigate this phenomenon. The main reason for the popularity of this phenomenon in the West was the desire of people to communicate with their dead relatives after World War I. In Indian mythology, telepathic communication has been mentioned at various places and at various times, and it is an accepted fact.

Telepathic communications spontaneously occur mainly at the time of crisis in the form of dreams, visions, feeling of something being wrong, clairaudience, popping up of images or words in the mind, etc. It appears that this phenomenon is related to emotions and intuition, and perhaps this is the reason why there are more cases involving women than men. After prolonged research at the Duke University in the 1930s, Professor Rhine concluded that clairvoyance and telepathy are basically the same, although their mode of manifestation is slightly different. He also observed that distance does not matter in telepathic communications. This was confirmed by the experiments conducted by an astronaut, Edgar D. Mitchell from Apollo 14 in 1971. He could successfully communicate certain numbers to his fellowmen on earth — some 150,000 miles away.

Psychics and mystics live in a different reality and they have easy access to various psychic abilities.

I remember an incident in 1959 when, after having completed my masters in mathematics, I was teaching in a college in North India. A psychic came to demonstrate his telepathic abilities. He stood near the blackboard with a chalk and a duster in his hand. He asked a person in the classroom to repeat each letter of his name in his mind.

The psychic said that he would also write those letters one by one. If he wrote a letter which was not correct, according to the name of the person, he should shake his head sideways. In that case, the psychic would write another letter and await confirmation. Within a few minutes, the psychic correctly wrote down the names of many individuals sitting there, without any apparent communication with anyone. This is an instance of telepathy and he told us that with regular practice, anyone could develop this ability. One could communicate an entire message to someone sitting in any part of the world.

If one believes in the existence of other worlds, I would recommend the book *On the Death of My Son* by Jasper Swain, who was a magistrate in South Africa at the time of writing the book. His son, after death, visited him in his astral forms and described the functioning of things in the other realm. According to him, telepathy and telekinesis are normal there.

Telekinesis or Psychokinesis (PK)
It is the movement of objects from one place to another without the use

of any physical force. The power of mental concentration can move objects, bend bars, twist spoons and forks and do many other similar things. Regular experiments have been conducted at the Duke University, and one can see things sliding within closed glass boxes due to the power of mind. Besides Professor J. B. Rhine, there have been other scientists who have either conducted experiments or witnessed this phenomenon. Some of them are, Nobel Prize winner Professor Brian Josephson; Professor Hans Bender of the

University of Freiberg, West Germany; Professor J. B. Hasted, Head of the Department of Physics, Birbeck College, London; Professor Charles Crussard of France and also Professor John G. Neihardt of the Department of English Literature at the University of Missouri, Columbia, who founded the Society for Research into Rapport and Telekinesis. Numerous cases of key bending, bending a screw placed inside a plastic tube, spoon twisting, etc., were demonstrated in public, before the learned scientists.

The term teleportation is used when an object passes through matter, or materialises on the table from nowhere. In the former case it is supposed that the object first dematerialises before entry into matter and then rematerialises after its passage through matter. In the latter case, the object disappears from one place and reappears at another. Yogic practices, in which deep breathing and intense concentration are combined, are also known to produce the effects of telekinesis.

Levitation

It is the phenomenon of rising into air, demonstrating the weightlessness of the body or the objects. A large number of cases of levitation have been reported from all over the world. Yogis and saints in the East and the West have, every now and then, demonstrated this psychic faculty. Christian saints have demonstrated this power for a long time. In the seventeenth century, Joseph of Cupertino was seen to levitate a number of times before several eyewitnesses. On one occasion he was in the air for about two hours. Simon Magus levitated from the top of the Roman Forum in the first century. However, St Peter stopped him, by praying to God, so as to put an end to such magical feats; as a result, Magus fell to the ground and was killed. Indian yogi Subbayah Pullavar achieved the gift of levitation after about twenty years of yoga practices. Many pictures showing him flying in the air appeared in the magazine *Illustrated London News* on June 6, 1936. Alexandra David Neel lived in Tibet for more than a decade and reported a variety of cases of levitation from there. A case of spontaneous levitation during rapture was witnessed when St Teresa of Avila rose one and a half foot above the ground for about half an hour.

Breathing and visualisation techniques in yoga are known to have provided paranormal powers known as *siddhis*, in Hinduism and Buddhism, including levitation. India has a large number of reported cases of levitation by such Brahmins. Many *fakirs* are known to have demonstrated their powers in this regard. For further information see the book *Tibetan Occult Science in India and Among the Ancients* by Louis Jacolliot (1971). Milarepa was a great yogi who was adept in levitation and was said to have many yogic powers. Many of his demonstrations, recorded in the thirteenth century, included walking or sleeping in the air.

In 1968, Daniel Dunglas Home levitated from a window on the third floor of the house and re-entered through another window. He demonstrated his ability to float in the air several times, in four decades. He could also levitate household objects. However, the Catholic Church did not respect his paranormal power and he was expelled. In the West, levitation has being considered as an evil act on many occasions. Many think that it is the act of ghosts, spirits and demons, and they consult an exorcist for a cure, if someone is seen to levitate. Several cases of demonic possessions have been recorded. People, beds, furniture and other objects are known to have floated in the air, causing immense trouble to those concerned. On the other hand, sceptics classify levitation as a fraud or hallucination.

It is perhaps only the Brahmins and Yogis of the East who categorise levitation as a positive paranormal power or *siddhi* and give a plausible explanation for it. According to them, *prana* or the 'vital fluid' has all powers latent in it. Through proper techniques of yoga and meditation, an adept person can control this power and use it for different purposes. According to them, although *prana* belongs to the spiritual world of non-material reality, it is also available in the physical world for all kinds of purposes and manifestations. A luminous aura is sometimes seen around saints when they levitate.

Yet the use of paranormal powers is forbidden in the yogic path to know Self/God. Yogis acquire the power(s), but they ignore it, for they might get caught in its attractions and may get misled from their noble mission. If, and only if, one has craving for God and nothing else, then one has the chances of knowing God. Attraction towards minor goals distracts one from the achievement of the major goal. For example, see my book, *Kundalini — An Autobiographical Guide to Self/God*

Realisation (1999). Once a practitioner came to Buddha and showed him his yogic achievements of twenty years. He concentrated and floated in air, crossed a river while in air and came back to Buddha successfully. He was feeling very proud and was expecting appreciation from him. Buddha told him that he had wasted his twenty years in vain; he could have paid a quarter of a rupee to the boatman who could have taken him across the river and brought him back. In twenty years, with the proper yogic approach, he could have broken the chain of reincarnations on earth to qualify to live on higher realms, where innumerable paranormal powers are natural. He could have achieved liberation.

Out-of-body Experiences (OBE)
Although it is a phenomenon which does not really fall in the category of paranormal experiences, yet it is customary to associate it with psychic phenomena. It is the dissociation of the person from the physical body and the subsequent travelling to distant places either in this world or the worlds of other

realities. Mostly the individual finds his/her self in a subtle body; which can be astral or etheric, or similar to the physical body, or a point or circle of light, or a dimensionless existence without any form. In the astral form, one may be clothed fully or partially or may be naked. Sometimes one may find the silver cord joining the astral body with the physical body, but it is not always so. The person travels with the speed of thought and one may find oneself disappearing from one place and reappearing at another. One is normally conscious of one's experience, whether it takes place while one is asleep or awake.

It is one phenomenon which I can very authentically describe since I have had such experiences, not once or twice but innumerable number of times, for more than a decade. It happened soon after the awakening of Kundalini in the year 1987. It is the result of the activation of the solar plexus or navel chakra, which is at the boundary between the lower world of physical nature and the spiritual worlds. In yogic traditions, it is believed that each chakra relates to experiences of its kind on activation. Activation of the navel chakra takes the person out of his/her physical body and makes him/her see the other realities. I suddenly found myself on one of the planes in a body which was similar to my physical body. Many times I flew with both my hands acting like the wings of a bird. I could stop at any place, descend to the ground, and see something which interested me, or talk to some person there, and then return to my flight again.

Once I found myself enclosed in a big hall, flying from one corner to

another and not finding a way out.
Suddenly an idea occurred to me —
I struck the wall with my body, and I
was out of the hall, experiencing a
feeling of being released from
confinement. I have flown over
colonies, similar to those on earth,
but the streets and buildings were
not crowded. Everywhere it was
neat and clean and I could see
gardens, parks, lakes, mountains,
etc. In later years, I found myself in a
dimensionless existence, having no
form, but a keen sense of awareness.
I had no hands or legs or any other
body part, but I could think and feel

as I did on earth. I could see many people walking on the ground, in the form of a point or a circle of light. Some of them were aware of my presence and were looking towards me. Perhaps there was some kind of light around me. I could see a translucent fortress in front of me and the beings there were entering from one gate and coming out from another. There were beautiful lakes, hills, trees laden with fruits, etc. The place seemed to be illuminated by some unknown source, since there was no sun or moon or electrification of any kind. A bluish green light was uniformly spread everywhere. I had a perpetual feeling of bliss and happiness and did not feel the need for anything at all.

Dr Carl Gustav Jung, the great psychologist of the West, also had out-of-body experiences towards the end of his life. It is unfortunate that he was always hindered by his quest for a scientific explanation for such phenomena and hence he could not delve deeper into them. However, his experience was spiritual in nature and he was full of bliss and happiness. Jung found himself floating "in a state of bliss thronged with the images of creation," and the physical world appeared "downright ridiculous" to him and seemed as a "segment of existence, enacted in a three dimensional box-like universe especially set up for it." In his own words, "I could never have imagined that any such experience was possible. It was not a product of imagination. The visions and experience were utterly real; there was nothing subjective about them; they all had the quality of absolute objectivity... We shy away from the word 'eternal', but I can describe the experience only as the ecstasy of a non-temporal state in which present, past and future are one" (Jung 1961, 275).

Evidence suggests that OBEs can also take place in a state of fear, stress, trauma, illness and hypnosis. While out of the body, people have none of the pain or suffering which they normally experience while in their physical bodies. According to some people, everyone has some kind of OBE during sleep; it is a different thing that such experiences are not regular and they have no ability to judge them. Some people report leaving their bodies through the solar plexus or the crown centre in the head, and returning through the same centre. According to some reports, when the soul leaves the body, it does so with a flopping sound, but when it returns to the body, it seems to melt into it. Some people see the silver cord connecting them to the physical bodies.

Many faiths and traditions believe in OBEs. In Hinduism and Buddhism it is known as *siddhi*, obtained as a result of yogic practices. The ancient Chinese also believed in such a phenomenon taking place during meditative practices. The Tibetan Book of the Dead talks about *bardo thodol* as the state of suspension beyond the physical realm. The ancient Egyptians believed that the soul of a person goes out of the body many times, but permanently goes out only at the time of death. However, they believed that one can return to one's body and so they preserved their bodies as *mummies* with all the physical amenities. Mithraic rites also centred round out-of-body experiences. Greek philosophers such as Socrates, Plato and Plotinus not only believed in out-of-body experiences, but they also gave a vivid description of their experiences in their writings. The Shamans could project themselves out-of-body after being in states of ecstasy.

Coming to methodical research on out-of-body experiences, the following notable persons are quotable. Marcel Louis Forhan and Robert A. Monroe had experienced out-of-body travels from early childhood. In their youth they consciously travelled out of their bodies and had encounters with women. Forhan married the woman he used to visit in astral form. Both Forhan and Monroe used to travel astrally with their women, who were also in their astral bodies, and enjoyed ecstatic astral sex. Sex on the astral level involved inflow of electrons and produced intense shocks. Forhan, who was later known as Yram, died in 1917. Yram believed that everyone can travel astrally and wrote the book *Practical Astral Travel*. Monroe described his adventures in the book *Journeys Out of the Body* (1971). He conducted regular research in his laboratory, which he later called Monroe Institute for Applied Sciences.

Monroe patented a sound which synchronised the left and right hemispheres of the brain, and was responsible for inducing sleep in the physical body, while the mind remained awake and alert. Monroe's approach was similar to that of Oliver Fox, who induced lucid dreaming with the body falling asleep, but the mind remaining awake. Fox's research around 1920 was later published as a book named *Astral Projection*. Duke

University and other laboratories have been experimenting with the phenomenon, but without any remarkable results. Some have reported out-of-body travels under the effect of marijuana, but this cannot be recommended as a healthy practice.

Aura

It is an egg-shaped field of vital energy that surrounds everything having an atomic structure. The size and brilliancy of the aura depends on the health and spirituality of the person. Arts and writings of ancient cultures such as India, Egypt,

Greece and Rome have invariably described the emanation of vital energy from various life forms. Pictures of saints and prophets from every culture have a halo around their heads which is either white or golden in colour. This is the depiction of the spiritual evolution they have achieved. It is said that the aura of Buddha extended to several miles; that is why so many people from neighbouring places were attracted to him. An average person has his or her aura extending to about eight or ten feet. Those in good health and/or those who are spiritually awakened have larger and brighter auras. Persons lacking good health or suffering from an illness of some kind have smaller and duller auras. By seeing the aura, one can find out not only the condition of one's health, but even the state of specific organs of the body, which may be suffering from a particular illness.

An aura cannot be seen by the naked eye. In 1919, Dr Walter J. Kilner developed a formula for aural diagnosis of illness. Semyon Davidovich Kirlian developed a kind of photography which could capture the auras on film. This was known as Kirlian photography in 1939. However, clairvoyants and yogis possess an extra sense beyond the five normal senses, and they are known to see and analyse the aura easily. According to Kilner, the aura had three main divisions:

- A dark and narrow space around the body, called *etheric double*

- Densest and constant-sized inner aura

- Outer aura of varying size which blends into the inner aura

Evidence shows that an aura has several layers. The first one is a layer of hazy or greyish matter, normally less than half-a-centimetre in thickness, called etheric double. This is also known as health aura, since the illness first appears in this part — days, weeks, months and sometimes even years before the physical manifestation of the disease. Around it there is a multi-coloured mist which fades away into space without having any specific boundary. The composition of this multicoloured mist varies and no two clairvoyants will have exactly the same opinion. In a broader sense, there are seven layers corresponding to seven bodies: physical, astral, mental, intuitional, *atmic*, monadic and divine. Then there are seven basic colours corresponding to seven basic chakras in the body: red (root), yellow (sacral), orange (solar plexus), green (heart), blue (throat), indigo (eyebrow) and violet (crown). Interpretations of colours may vary from person to person according the system one follows. One can also know the past, present and future through a reading of aura. Through practice, one can learn how to see and read auras. For complete details one can refer to my book on Aura in the same series.

Mediumship

It is a very practical psychic phenomenon, in which the medium comes in contact with the alleged non-physical entities, be it the spirit of a dead relative, a demi-god, a spirit guide or God Himself. One channelises the universal life force through himself or herself, which can be used for a variety of purposes, such as healing, talking to dead relatives, etc. Various names have been given to such people, but the central line of action is one and the same, that is, energy from the beyond works through the medium: the medium has no power of his or her own.

There are two main categories: physical and mental. In the physical category, there is a movement of objects in different forms, such as telekinesis, levitation, etc. Hundreds and thousands of such cases are well-known in many Asian and Western countries. When the medium of communication is mental, the communication takes place through inner vision and hearing, automatic writing or speech. Although the parap-sychologists and sceptics say that it is some psychic part of the medium himself or herself, nevertheless, a large number of believers have always existed who take the results at face value.

The gift of mediumship, like any other psychic ability, is more pronounced in most people in their childhood, and is generally suppressed by the so-called intelligent and scientific adult world. It is related to sentiments and intuition and this is the reason why most of the mediums, especially in the West, have been women. At one time, there was a flood of housewives-turned mediums in the USA and the UK, and many of them charged money for their sessions on a professional basis. I will describe some cases I personally know to be true, which validate this phenomenon.

Stephen O'Brien who lives in Swansea, England, has authored three wonderful books, two of them being, *Visions of Another World* and *Voices from Heaven* (O'Brien 1989). He spoke at a gathering of several hundred people in a hall and talked to them one by one, guided by a spirit from the higher realm. As the spirit told him about some person sitting on a particular seat and having a particular name, Stephen would call the person by name and would convey the details of the message as seen by him in the vision or as told by the spirit. Both the person and the spirit recognised each other and could talk to each other through Stephen. This is a firsthand proof of the existence of life beyond physical death, and any one can go and try it personally. Stephen visits other realms in his subtle body and has talked with several entities there; accounts of these visits are given in his book. Another book that I recommend is *We Are Not Forgotten* by Martin and Romanowski (1991). However, there are hundreds of such books that are flooding the market today.

Another personal experience I have repeatedly felt is that of talking to my father, who left the physical world in September 1992. I communicate with the spirit of my father through a medium living in Ashville, North Carolina. The medium goes into a trance, that is, he puts himself aside to make way for the spirit from beyond. And then the spirit talks to me through him. I first talked to my father in 1995, three years after his demise. He told me that he was recovering from his fractured leg in a kind of hospital. He said that he was finally at rest after a long time. His thinking had changed and he looked at things in an entirely different way. Soon he was to get a new body and he was to be transferred to a more lighted area. He wanted his things in the house in Delhi to be removed, and requested that people should not disturb him emotionally, so that he would not be distracted from the path of progress. He asked me to convey this message to his wife, that is, my mother. He said he was sorry that I was not present when he had left the world and that he would like to embrace me once.

I talked with my father again in June 2000, when I had come to attend the annual conference of our Academy of Religion and Psychical Research in Philadelphia. He told me he was in a higher realm and had a light body. He could have had a full body if and whenever he wanted. When I asked him if and when he would have his next incarnation, he said he never thought about it and time had no meaning in that reality. They just lived in the 'now' and there were many teachers who visited them and imparted knowledge. He said there were many wonderful colours there, which he had never seen on earth. "We are never hungry or thirsty and we never talk about food over here," he said.

There cannot be conclusive evidence of life after death in the scientific manner of repeatable experiments. At the Duke University, which has been researching on psychic phenomena since early 1920, there is no scientific equation to prove the existence of such a phenomenon. However, individuals will always have individual proofs in one way or the other, and they would not care for what science says.

Healing (Psychic or Spiritual)
It is the phenomenon of healing a person by treating his or her illness with the help of an energy whose source is beyond the physical realm, without the use of any curative

agent of physical nature. Although there are several names given to this kind of healing, the process is the same, that is, to invoke the spiritual energy through prayer or meditation and direct it towards the patient. Almost all psychic healers admit that it is not they who are healing, rather it is the spirit from the higher realm which heals.

Psychic surgery is beyond belief until you see it personally. The surgeon inserts his hands into the body of the patient and removes the defective part(s). The surface operated on remains smooth and the blood stains can be wiped off with a cloth. In a few minutes the patient can walk home, smiling. There is no anaesthesia used. I have personally seen such cases and have met people who have undergone such operations successfully. Antonio Agpaoa of the Philippines, better known as Tony, was perhaps the most famous person with this ability. He used to cure about 300 people in a day. There was no fixed fee: you could donate whatever you felt like, from a penny to a million dollars. Tony used to go into a momentary trance to invite the 'vital energy' from the cosmos, which used to do everything, as he always smilingly said.

Psychic healing is done in various ways. Although one uses spiritual energy, it is not necessary for the patient to have faith. Nevertheless, the healers normally have a strong religious faith, which they use for invoking the 'universal life force'. Illness or disease is caused by a depletion or imbalance of this life force by factors such as poor diet, negative thinking, etc. The healer gets this balance restored by transferring the *prana* or the universal life force from beyond, into the patient, either directly or through himself or herself. The force may be passed through touch, or motion of the hand over the body of the patient or even from a long distance. The patient feels the infusion of energy and there can be sensations of shock, tingling, heat, etc. Both in psychic surgery and shamanism, the healer extracts an object out of the body of the patient, which supposedly has been the cause of illness. Whether to believe in it or not depends on the patient and the onlookers.

I have witnessed such phenomena, where objects are extracted in a similar fashion. My relative had a stone in her gall bladder, which had been troubling her for quite some time. She was afraid of the operation. On knowing about a person who had the power of extracting stones without any operation, we drove overnight to that place and the patient stood in the queue, which had about 50 patients. The healer removed the stones of all the patients in about an hour's time. He would move his hand from a distance over the gall bladder or kidney of the patient, holding a fresh leaf of some tree and say something. In a moment the stone would fall to the ground. The patient would collect the stone and go away, making room for others. Many people got the stone tested in the laboratory and found calcium in it. Some patients felt an emptiness or a slight pain in the portion that used to hold the stone, but it disappeared in a few days. Many other scientists saw this with me. None of us had any doubts about it, whether anybody else in the world believes in it or not. In fact, India is known for yogis and people with miraculous powers, and this kind of healing is just a small drop in the ocean. Generally, people are born with such powers, but the powers can also be attained through practice. Yogis possess many psychic powers, but they seldom make use of them.

The scientific community of the world, and the sceptics, do not and will not believe in the psychic powers of healing, although there has been some change in this situation after the developments in quantum physics. Nevertheless, psychics, healers, shamans, yogis, etc., have continued working with the universal life force and they make use of it in different ways. People in both categories may be right in their own ways. I can say so because I am both, a scientist and a yogi. As a scientist you may not believe in what is happening, but as a yogi experiencing it personally, you tend to believe in it. Science may not believe in it because it has not yet reached that stage of development. According to science the universe is dead matter, but according to healers and yogis the universe is a living entity, where everyone and everything is mutually connected. However, successful healing requires certain conditions.

- Faith in the process on the part of both the healer and the patient. Sceptics can be so negative at times that the healing may not take place. A feeling of guilt and acceptance of illness as punishment can also be an obstacle. According to yoga there are no sins, only causes and their effects. If one learns from one's mistakes and does not repeat them then the sin is washed off.

- Compassion for the patient on one hand, and petition to the higher power on the other, are necessary requirements on the part of the healer.

- The healer and the patient should be in tune with each other, so as to create an atmosphere of relaxation.

- Places where the universal life force is present in abundance, bring quick success. Such places are elevated areas, such as hills or mountains; and where water is present, especially fresh water.

Parts of a house or particular rooms which are kept clean and where prayers are offered, are better places for obtaining quick results.

Although people are born with psychic powers, nevertheless, one can also acquire them with regular practice. Evidence shows that healers go in another reality, called the 'altered state of consciousness', from where the *prana* or *energy* acts on the patient. Such a state is similar to the mystical state, but it is not the same. Many healers claim that others can learn the art of going into from them. Finally, one should remember that Jesus cured 10 people, but only 7 were healed. Hence one should not expect hundred per cent results.

Prophecy

It is a prediction of the highest order, which concerns humanity at large. In fact it is different from ordinary predictions or precognitions, as forthcoming universal events are revealed in one form or the other to highly evolved souls. Prophets or great persons such as the Buddha, Jesus and Mohammed were divinely chosen to preach the divine message to the masses. The collective unconscious is the storehouse of all happenings, which are psychically read by the conscious Self of an enlightened personality. People go into a trance in states of ecstasy, which can be induced by various methods. Scriptures of ancient civilisations such as Indian, Hebrew, early Christian, Greek, Egyptian, Chinese, etc., are full of prophetic revelations.

In modern times also, there have been a large number of individuals who were psychic. In the sixteenth century, Nostradamus, on the basis of certain revelations predicted major future events — most of which have come true. He used to see future events effortlessly and considered them to be the will of God. Several scholars have researched on a large number of quatrains written by Nostradamus. At the turn of the last century, we had Edgar Cayce, who is credited with about fifteen thousand trance readings. He could easily see the past, too, and advised individuals about why certain things were happening to him or her. Elizabeth

Claire Prophet could see several thousand years back in the past and hence she described the voluminous and intricate details of the lost civilisation of Atlantis and the Mayan culture. She has given details about future events, too. Paul Twitchell of Eckankar claims that he has described the future for several millenniums, surpassing the details given by Nostradamus. He has prophesied the merger of science and religion in the twenty-first century. Many people had prophesied the assassination of President John F. Kennedy.

Ecstasy

This is the ultimate level of psychic development, which explodes like a volcanic eruption. As a culmination of one's life-long practices, when a person comprehends the Absolute, one bursts into a condition of inner happiness and bliss. Although the realisation of the ultimate reality varies according to one's faith and grooming, the accompaniment of blissfulness is nearly the same. It has rightly been called the 'psychology of joy' by the Jungian philosopher, Robert A. Johnson (1987). Johnson described the Greek god Dionysus, who could bring transcendent joy or madness, as the personification of divine ecstasy. Dionysus is the personification of wine, which has the ability to bring either spiritual transcendence or physical addiction. After having realised the ultimate reality, several Hindu, Christian and Sufi saints have been known to dance with joy, forgetting the world around them. For example, see the life histories of various saints — Kabir, Tulsidas, Meerabai, Jalaluddin Rumi, Meister Eckhart, and Teresa de Avila, etc. They experienced the presence of God with a beatific vision.

One loses one's individual identification once one has attained the state of inner peace and calmness that accompanies oneness with God, as described in *Aham Brahmasmi* or *I Am That I Am*. Such a state of blissfulness has no conception of time. It varies from person to person. On an average it lasts for half-an-hour. Sufi saint, Meherbaba was once lost in such a state for about four to five days. He did not know what clothes he was wearing or if he had any food to eat in that state of divine intoxication. The Hindu saint, Meerabai was perhaps always in such a state of blissfulness, for months together. She invariably said that her lover Krishna was always with her and she did not want any other thing. In such a state she drank the poison given to her by her husband, who did not like her to constantly harbour thoughts of another male, be it Lord Krishna Himself. But the poison did not harm her at all. In Indian mythology there have been child saints like Dhruva and Prahlada, who were always in the state of divine intoxication. They were thrown from the tops of hills;

enclosed in rooms with poisonous snakes; elephants were made to walk over them and they were even thrown into the sea, but nothing happened to them.

Ecstasy is a state of trance in which the limbs become rigid and breathing and circulation slow down to a minimum. It can well be compared with the unconscious state of patients under the influence of some anaesthetic in a hospital. In terms of psychology it is the 'unification of consciousness', the Zen masters call it 'centring' and Abraham H. Maslow referred to it as a 'peak experience'. According to Maslow, an exceptional individual who has satisfied all his or her lower needs, is the one who realises his or her full potential, leading to self-actualisation. It is a 'carrying away' sensation and some persons are literally known to have levitated, for example Saint Teresa of Avila and John of the Cross. Ramakrishna Paramahansa used to enter into ecstatic states through the slightest of divine provocations such as hearing the name of God in any form like Ram, Allah or by seeing any place of worship, etc.

Psychic Individuation

In everybody's life there comes a
stage when s/he begins to
understand the meaninglessness of
life. All worldly goals begin to
appear as if they are of no real use.
The person begins to nurture a
feeling that s/he lives in this world
but s/he does not belong to it.
Various objects and processes for
sense gratification begin to appear
useless, as they do not lead
anywhere. The person feels that
s/he has wasted a lifetime in useless

pursuits and begins to look for something which can give everlasting happiness and inner peace. The person begins to feel that s/he has forgotten his/her real identity, in some way or the other, and has lost touch with his/her roots. S/he begins to feel that s/he belongs somewhere else and looks for means to find that place, his/her real home. This is the beginning of the search for Self or *Atman*, which is the only permanent element in the whole universe. Dr Carl Jung called it the 'longing for psychic individuation'.

The psychic development of a person takes place in five distinct stages. In the first stage, one remains engrossed in various means of sense gratification and one has no regard for the feelings of others. For the individual at this stage, maximisation of physical pleasure is the only reality on earth. There is no inkling of any higher power beyond earth. In the second stage, one begins to feel that there is some higher power, but one continues to remain engrossed in various means of sense gratification in different ways. In the third stage, the feeling that there is a higher power becomes firmer, and one begins to take part in various rituals in order to please that Supreme Power for achieving worldly goals and objects. One begins to believe in God, but has no consideration for the views of others and continues to avoid responsibility. In the fourth stage, equal importance is given to what others believe in or think, and one begins to take responsibility. One begins to feel that simply taking part in rituals will not lead anywhere, and one must look for a concrete means of knowing the truth. It is the beginning of the inner turmoil. In the fifth stage, one fully appreciates the meaninglessness of life and the inner turmoil precipitates a search for truth in the consciousness. One begins to join various societies or academies that are pursuing the same goal, in an organised way. One also begins to take interest in scriptures and/or authentic writings related to the search of truth or God, and for this one may adopt some solid means of approach such as yoga, meditation, etc. Dr Joel L. Whitton and Joe Fisher call the five stages — Materialism,

Superstition, Fundamentalism, Philosophy and Inner Turmoil.

Awakening

Awakening means a new awareness or the opening of one's eyes to a new reality, which was not known to the person earlier. According to Dr Carl Jung there is a 'Higher Unifying Centre' called 'Higher Self', which one may come to know about at the time of awakening. Sri Aurobindo called it the Psychic Being and defined it as a separate personality — developed around one's soul, in the course of several lives. This Higher Self or Psychic Being mediates between the Soul and God, and spiritual enlightenment is experienced.

Usually, before the awakening is experienced, a problem such as some dissatisfaction or disappointment, a feeling that something is missing in life, a feeling of guilt and self-responsibility, etc., has to be resolved. At such a juncture one may or may not understand the real meaning of the problem. If one does not understand the real meaning of the problem, one becomes even more miserable and may curse oneself or put the blame on God. But if one understands rightly, then there is an end to all suffering. Development in the right direction brings spiritual experiences such as seeing inner lights, hearing inner sounds, having visions. Many people have their talents enhanced, for example, a writer may become more prolific and may write intuitively about things that are not rationally known. The personality undergoes a complete transformation. People may have one or more of the psychic experiences described in the previous section. One achieves inner security, calm, power, serenity, blissfulness, clear understanding and unconditional love that radiates for everyone.

Balancing Masculinity and Femininity

Every individual, male or female, has elements of both masculinity and femininity, which require a balancing for psychic individuation. Masculinity implies intellectuality, rationality, action, etc.; while femininity implies emotionality, intuition, passive reception, etc. Innumerable lifetimes are spent in achieving this balance. Whenever this balance is achieved, one has completed the process of individuation or graduation from the school of earth. So, one can see how important it is to acquire such a balance. All great people possessed this exceptional quality. A very good example is that of King David of the Old Testament. When his son challenged him for the possession of the kingdom, he fought miraculously and defeated him. However, when his son died, he wept so bitterly that he was about to lose the battle. His general was a wise man with a magnificent personality, who took care of the situation and the king, and David won the battle. An individuated person is supposed to have enough courage and strength to fight the battle of life, and at the same time, enough sentiments and compassion to give unconditional love to others.

Every male has an *inner woman*, which attracts him towards outer or physical women. The man selects a woman for marriage or companion-ship, if she matches the image of the woman in his mind at that time. After some time he finds that she does not match his requirements, for one reason or the other, and looks for another woman. He takes another woman and after some time the same story is repeated. The whole life is frittered away like this and the same story continues in the next lifetime too. The man remains eternally dissatisfied and the chain of incarnations continues. The same thing applies to women. They remain dissatisfied in their lives with the men they live with, and the story continues in the following lifetimes. The chain of reincarnations breaks once and for all when the secret is learnt that it is not the outer woman or man who is giving you dissatisfaction, but it is your own inner man or woman.

Inner woman is, in fact, related to the surroundings, especially to women, but the man is not aware of this fact. Jung called the inner woman *anima* and the inner man *animus*. Jung's successor Dr Esther Harding has written a voluminous book on this subject, *Women's Mysteries*. Anima in the man looks for satisfaction in the form of a physical woman, a wife, a girlfriend or a female in some significant relationship. He goes on throughout his life trying to find the woman of his imagination. He selects the one who suits his requirements to the best approximation at that point of time. He thinks that he has found his soulmate and begins life with her. He does not understand the trick of the anima and the relationship falls apart. He goes for another woman and the same story is repeated. The courts are filled with cases of divorce for this reason only. With repeated experiences of this kind, the man finally becomes a misogynist. Some people even develop psychological problems. Exactly the same thing applies to women too. They also remain sexually dissatisfied, because even they have been looking for some kind of satisfaction in men, which cannot be found in them. The animus tries to match the requirement of the psyche of the woman with the outer man, and the same mistake is repeated as in the case of anima. Women, too, are known to develop a hatred for men or some other psychological disorder.

It is not that man and woman should not live with each other; in fact they are complementary to each other and have been created to live with each other. However, their aims and objectives differ so much that it does not take much time for the relationship to fall apart. All of us have male and female elements within ourselves, which are in perpetual conflict with each other within the psyche. As long as this conflict is not settled, no satisfactory relation is possible. The individuals should look inward, analyse their psyche, recognise the reason(s) for imbalance and adopt means to remove this imbalance. It is the lack of wholeness within one's own psyche, which is the cause of dissatisfaction. That is why saints, prophets or spiritually elevated persons have a calm, satisfied, pleasant smile on their faces, since they have achieved wholeness. They do not need an outer woman or man.

The complementary nature of man and woman should be understood properly. Domestic and official duties should be divided between the two. It is not that the man should keep looking for a new physical woman every time the circumstances or environment around him changes. One has to stop following the anima projection of the outer woman blindly. This blind following will not end in this life but will follow life after life, as a childish phase. Once man has controlled his impulsive attraction towards the physical woman, has learnt to sacrifice the sexual instinct and is able to withdraw from the woman who attracts him, then he begins to understand the cause of death and rebirth. This is a sort of initiation into a spiritual life, a conquest of sexual desires, which comes after several incarnations of perfecting oneself through a variety of personal experiences. One is liberated from the binding forces of *maya*. Once this inner relation is balanced, there is no need for an outer relationship; it becomes a matter of convenience and personal choice, without compulsions of any kind. Similarly, a woman has to make herself perfect from within, if she wants to have a successful relationship with a man.

Not that all saints have been single, rather a larger number of them have been married, but they had no complaints against their

spouses. Once three well-known
saints met at the temple of Tirupati
in India. The first one was happily
married and he thanked God for
providing him with such a wife who
could be instrumental in his Self-
realisation. The second saint had a
wife who always fought with him
and there was no peace at home; he
thanked God for providing him
with such a wife, who forced him to
find peace elsewhere, which he
finally found in God. The third saint
had never married and remained
single all his life; he thanked God for
circumstances in which he could

never come in contact with a woman, so that he could realise the Self/God. So you see, the three saints in unique and entirely different situations in life achieved the same kind of Self-realisation. This means that it is not the outer woman or man which has anything to do with God-realisation; it is the inner woman or man with whom one has to get married.

When this 'inner marriage' takes place an 'inner child' is born who represents the culmination of inner experiences. It is the *holy child* of the Chinese and the *psychic child* of parapsychologists. It represents perfection within the individual. Such an individual has achieved a unification of the opposite pairs, a balance between the male and female principles and has graduated from the school of earth. There are no more incarnations for him/her any more. This is what Lord Jesus meant when he said, "When the two become one, and male with female neither male nor female…". This is the reason that the Hindus say, "What need we have of children, we who have this Self…?" It is the proof of psychic individuation being achieved. And one sees that inner child in a very clear way in the twilight period just before falling asleep or on just coming out of sleep. I remember the beautiful child with an innocent smile who appeared in my dream on the night of January 1, 1988 in London; and again the next morning in a different pose.

A man or a woman at this stage becomes a complete unit in himself or herself and roams freely around the world with no pressing needs whatsoever. A single eye watching you from a distance, either in a dream or a vision, also indicates initiation into spiritual life. This is your Higher Self telling you that you should now give up all worldly pursuits to move further on the path of spiritual life.

Individuation and Dreams

Not only Freud and Jung but Indian yogis, Egyptian and Chinese masters too have laid stress on the importance of dreams. Dreams are found to follow an arrangement or pattern, called the *process of individuation* by Jung. It appears that there is a hidden regulating or directing force at work, which is responsible for the imperceptible process of psychic growth. With the maturity of man's relationship with woman, the anima also matures, and the psychic level of the females appearing in dreams rises from the lowest to the highest. According to Swami Satyananda Saraswati, energy at different levels is known as:

- Ignorance
- Sex
- Love
- Spiritual experience

Accordingly, anima females represent the level of psychic

growth in dreams in the following successive stages:

- Ignorance, symbolised by a primitive woman such as Eve
- Sex, symbolised by a romantic beauty such as Cleopatra
- Love, symbolised by the Virgin Mary
- Spiritual experience, symbolised by Athena — the Greek goddess of wisdom or goddess Durga or Mona Lisa — with her mysterious smile

In the mechanical life of today, the fourth stage of psychic development is not easy to reach, but at the same time it is not impossible either. Ramakrishna witnessed the presence of Mother Goddess. I also witnessed the appearance of Mother Goddess blessing me with her right hand, three times in a period of about two months in 1987. Animus males also appear in the dreams of women in the following stages:

- Ignorance , represented by a primitive man such as Tarzan

- Sex, represented by a romantic man such as the poet Shelley

- Love, symbolised by the bearer of the torch, for example, Lloyd George

- Spiritual experience, symbolised by a guide to spiritual truth such as Mahatma Gandhi.

The guiding force behind all these experiences is the Self or *Atman*, which also supervises the psychic development, as a witness or onlooker, in different ways. The initial encounter with the 'inner friend' or Self is in some way the wounding of the personality. It is like the visiting card that the Self presents to us. Gradually when we know the Self, it helps us and communicates with us in different ways. For example, it may appear as an outstanding personality in a dream and might convey some message to us. This is how I had seen my Higher Self — talking to me in dreams. The Self is our shadow, which represents our unconscious ambition as a successful character in dreams. Sometimes the shadow represents those qualities, that we dislike in others, and which is the opposite side of ego. For example, I have sometimes seen myself beating someone with a cane or a rod. It may be because I do not like one of my brothers beating his wife and children in that way in real life.

Therefore, we have to learn to differentiate between the Self and our own shadow, in dreams.

One can also clearly differentiate between the Self and anima/animus. Self normally appears as an outstanding personality of the same sex, while anima/animus appears as an average personality of the opposite sex. However, both Self and anima/animus are there only to help us and guide us to grow spiritually towards perfection. For greater details one can refer to my book on Kundalini (Kumar 1999).

Salvation or Self-realisation

There is a phenomenal ego or personal self that deals with the affairs of the phenomenal world, and a Self or *Atman* which is akin to God. The Huna code of the lost Polynesian culture talks about the self at three levels: the low self, the middle self and the high self. The low self is the phenomenal ego, the middle self is the Self or *Atman*, and high self is the individualised personality living outside the physical body of the person. The final formation of the high self takes place in two stages: in the first place the male and female aspects of the personality have to be united in a single middle self, and then the three selves — low, middle and high — are to be united in the high self, thus creating a new high self. The three levels of the self (low, middle and high) pass through several incarnations (perhaps a dozen) before becoming the new high self, representing the unification of the opposite pairs. The union is never broken and the high self thus formed graduates to the next higher level of high self, and then the next, and so on, getting closer to God with each graduation.

Mainstream Christianity advocates three steps to salvation: crucifixion, death and resurrection, and this is an unrepeatable event. According to Gnostics, salvation or liberation is an ongoing process, both on earth and on higher realms. The Huna code of the Polynesians, Hinduism, Sufism and Buddhism, Corpocrates and Paul — all of them believed in the continuous process of liberation, spanning a number of lifetimes. Crucifixion means the inner turmoil which makes the individual lose interest in the common goals of the world and take interest in serious methods, such as yoga and meditation or intellectual metaphysics. Death of ego is the culmination of the search for truth by any method adopted by the practitioner. Resurrection is the awakening, to a new reality following death of ego, as described in the earlier section. Those who are on the right path continue to evolve endlessly on higher realms, even after breaking the cycle of death and rebirth in the physical world.

Glossary

akashic	pertaining to the sky
shamans	a doctor-priest or medicine man working by magic
fakirs	mendicant, a religious beggar regarded as a holy man
mummies	embalmed or otherwise preserved dead bodies
maya	illusion

OTHER TITLES IN THE SERIES